Jungle Animals

Series Editor Deborah Lock
US Senior Editor Shannon Beatty
Editor Arpita Nath
Senior Art Editor Ann Cannings
Art Editor Yamini Panwar
Senior Producer, Pre-production Nikoleta Parasaki
Picture Researcher Sakshi Saluja
Jacket Designer Charlotte Jennings
DTP Designers Ashok Kumar and Dheeraj Singh
Managing Editor Soma B. Chowdhury
Managing Art Editor Ahlawat Gunjan
Art Director Martin Wilson

Reading Consultant
Linda Gambrell, Ph.D.

First American Edition, 2016
Published in the United States by DK Publishing
345 Hudson Street, New York, New York 10014

16 17 18 19 20 10 9 8 7 6 5 4 3 2 1
001—285392—June/16

A catalog record for this book is available
from the Library of Congress.

ISBN: 978-1-4654-4962-7 (Paperback)
ISBN: 978-1-4654-4963-4 (Hardback)

DK books are available at special discounts when purchased in bulk for sales promotions,
premiums, fund-raising, or educational use. For details, contact:
DK Publishing Special Markets
345 Hudson Street, New York, New York 10014
SpecialSales@dk.com

Printed and bound in China.

The publisher would like to thank the following for their kind permission to reproduce their photographs:
(Key: a=above, b=below/bottom, c=center, l=left, r=right, t=top)
1 Getty Images: Anup Shah. **4 Dorling Kindersley:** Whipsnade Zoo, Bedfordshire (cra). **5 Philip Dowell:** (crb).
Dreamstime.com: Eric Isselee (cl). **Science Photo Library:** John Mitchell (tc). **6 naturepl.com:** Jack Dykinga (bl).
6–7 Corbis: Jim Zuckerman. **8–9 naturepl.com:** Roland Seitre. **10–11 Corbis:** DLILLC. **12–13 Corbis:** Kevin Kurek/dpa.
14-15 naturepl.com: Pete Oxford. **16-17 Alamy Images:** Design Pics Inc. **18-19 Getty Images:** heatherwest. **19 Robert
Harding Picture Library:** Frans Lanting (c). **20-21 Getty Images:** Clara Zamith. **22 Alamy Images:** Design Pics Inc (bl);
Arco Images GmbH (cla). **Dreamstime.com:** Eric Isselee (clb); Rinus Baak (cl). **24 naturepl.com:** Jack Dykinga (bl)
Endpapers: **Dorling Kindersley:** Frank Greenaway. **Jacket credits:** *Front:* **Getty:** Heather West (c), Andy Rouse (tc). **dk.com:**
Jerry Young (cl). *Back:* **dk.com:** Dave King, Courtesy of Whipsnade Zoo, Bedfordshire (tl)

All other images © Dorling Kindersley
For further information see: www.dkimages.com

A WORLD OF IDEAS:
SEE ALL THERE IS TO KNOW

www.dk.com

Contents

Enter the jungle,
if you dare!
Look up! Look down!
Look out!

Parrots

A parrot flies
over the jungle.
Its feathers flash red,
yellow, green, and blue.

feathers

Toucans

berry

beak

A toucan picks
a berry with
its large, long beak.

Orangutans swing from tree to tree. They move very quickly.

Sun Bears

Sun bears climb
the trees.
Their long claws
grip the branches.

claw

Giant Anteaters

snout

An anteater sniffs
an ants' nest
with its long snout.

ants' nest

Tarantulas

ground

A tarantula feels
the ground shake
with its hairy legs.

hairy legs

Tigers

A tiger hides
in the grass.
It watches and waits,
ready to leap.

Jaguars

A jaguar rests.
Ssh!
Quiet in the jungle,
please!

Glossary

Beak
hard, pointed
bird's mouth

Claws
sharp, curved
toe-points

Feathers
soft covering
on bird's body

Snout
long, pointed nose
and mouth used
to smell and eat

Spider's legs
hairy body parts
used to move and
sense animals nearby

Index

23

A Note to Parents

DK Readers is a four-level interactive reading adventure series for children, designed in conjunction with leading literacy experts, including Dr. Linda Gambrell, Distinguished Professor of Education at Clemson University. Dr. Gambrell has served as President of the National Reading Conference, the College Reading Association, and the International Reading Association.

Beautiful illustrations and superb full-color photographs combine with engaging, easy-to-read stories to offer a fresh approach to each subject in the series. Each DK Reader is guaranteed to capture a child's interest while developing his or her reading skills, general knowledge, and love of reading.

The four levels of DK Readers are aimed at different reading abilities, enabling you to choose the books that are exactly right for your child:

Level 1: Learning to read
Level 2: Beginning to read
Level 3: Beginning to read alone
Level 4: Reading alone

The "normal" age at which a child begins to read can be anywhere from three to eight years old. Adult participation through the lower levels is very helpful for providing encouragement, discussing storylines, and sounding out unfamiliar words.

No matter which level you select, you can be sure that you are helping your child learn to read, then read to learn!